HOW TO INCREASE PHONEMIC AWARENESS IN THE CLASSROOM

Lynn Settlow
Margarita Jacovino

ScarecrowEducation
Lanham, Maryland • Toronto • Oxford
2004

KH

Published in the United States of America
by ScarecrowEducation
An imprint of The Rowman & Littlefield Publishing Group, Inc.
4501 Forbes Boulevard, Suite 200, Lanham, Maryland 20706
www.scarecroweducation.com

PO Box 317
Oxford
OX2 9RU, UK

Copyright © 2004 by Lynn Settlow and Margarita Jacovino

British Library Cataloguing in Publication Information Available

Library of Congress Cataloging-in-Publication Data

Settlow, Lynn
   How to increase phonemic awareness in the classroom / Lynn Settlow,
Margarita Jacovino.
      p. cm.
   Includes bibliographical references and index.
   ISBN 1-57886-153-5 (pbk. : alk. paper)
   1. English language—Phonemics—Study and teaching
(Elementary)—Activity programs. 2.
Reading—Phonetic method—Activity programs. I. Jacovino, Margarita
II. Title.
LB1573.3.S48 2004
372.46'5—dc22

                                                   2004003434

∞™ The paper used in this publication meets the minimum requirements of
American National Standard for Information Sciences—Permanence of
Paper for Printed Library Materials, ANSI/NISO Z39.48-1992.
Manufactured in the United States of America.

12/21/06

To our students, past, present, and future,
who have been our inspiration and
taught us so much along the way.

CONTENTS

ACKNOWLEDGMENTS

Margo: I would like to thank my mother, my family, and my fiancé, Joseph, for their love, encouragement, and support. I cherish each and every one of you and love you from the bottom of my heart.

Lynn: I would also like to thank my friends and family for their love and support.

Special thanks to Judy Rothman and Tom Koerner for their assistance. We would also like to thank Valerie Portny, Dolores Perin, Susan Masullo, Eileen Marzola, and the Churchill School and Center.

INTRODUCTION

The day a child enters nursery school, and often before, parents and teachers share a common concern. How can we help this child learn to read? What do we need to do to prepare him or her? This leads to the next logical question: What is the best method of instruction for teaching reading? The reading war between whole language and phonics instruction in recent education history illustrates the importance—and controversy—of these questions. In recent years, a pair of new phrases has been added to the mix, *phonemic awareness* and *phonological awareness*. Teachers and parents alike have gotten the message: these are necessary skills for reading. This has only led to new questions. What exactly is phonemic awareness? How do we teach it? Where do we start and where do we stop? *How to Increase Phonemic Awareness in the Classroom* will answer these questions for you while providing a phonemic awareness curriculum that is easy to follow.

PHONOLOGICAL AND PHONEMIC AWARENESS

There are a few terms that need defining before we go further. The terms in this book fall under the umbrella of *metalinguistic awareness*, which is the ability to reflect on the features of spoken language. A person can think about and control their use of language separately from thinking about its actual meaning. *Phonological awareness* is a component of metalinguistic awareness, and reflects the capability to hear and manipulate large units of sound, such as syllables, *onsets*, and *rimes*. Put simply, onsets are the consonants that precede the first vowel in a word. Rimes are the first vowel in a word and all the letters that come after it. For example, in the word *train*, /tr/ is the onset and /ain/ is the rime. In the word *game*, /g/ is the onset and /ame/ is the rime. Rimes should not be confused with the common term "rhyme."

Phonemic awareness is a component of phonological awareness, just as phonological awareness is a component of metalinguistic awareness. Phonemic awareness reflects the ability to hear and manipulate phonemes, which are the smallest units of sound that make up the speech stream. Despite the distinction between the two domains, the terms phonological and phonemic awareness are often used interchangeably. Since the goal of the book is to target and develop phonemic awareness, we use the term phonemic awareness exclusively from this point.

As stated above, phonemes are the smallest units of sound in the speech stream. There are 44 phonemes in the English language, albeit only 26 letters. This is because there are differences between short and long vowels as well as sounds attributed to consonant and vowel digraphs (/ch/ in *chair*, /oi/ in *boil*, etc.). Phonemes are abstract and sometimes difficult to hear. The difference between the sounds of two phonemes can be subtle, but it changes the meaning of words. For example, the sounds /b/ and /p/ are very similar, but when attached to the beginning of words like *bat* and *pat* these similar sounds create two different words.

A person possessing phonemic awareness can identify and segment sounds in the spoken word. For example, he knows that there are three sounds in the word *bat* (b-a-t), three sounds in the word *same* (s-a-me), and four sounds in the word *clock* (c-l-o-ck). However, experts are quick to point out that it is not just hearing the difference between two phonemes that matters. It is the awareness that these sounds can be manipulated, added, and transposed in words that matters most. Children with phonemic awareness can also blend strings of isolated sounds together to form recognizable words. They can add /c/ to *lock* to form the word *clock*, then replace /cl/ with /s/ to form the word *sock*. They can segment the word *mop* into three sounds (m-o-p) and if asked could say the word backward (*pom*).

Phonemic awareness skills are best viewed as part of a developmental continuum. The beginning skill is recognizing and subsequently generating rhymes, followed by alliteration, blending, segmenting, and finally manipulating phonemes. Students need to work their way up to being able to manipulate individual sounds. It is easier to blend and segment larger sounds, such as syllables and onsets and rimes, than it is to blend and segment individual phonemes. By the end of nursery school, most children can recognize rhymes and alliteration. By the end of kindergarten, most children can generate rhymes, break words into syllables, and remove the first syllable from a multisyllabic word. By the completion of first grade, most children can identify and manipulate phonemes.

THE IMPORTANCE OF PHONEMIC AWARENESS

Why the sudden interest in phonemic awareness and why does all this matter? While educational researchers have been aware of phonemic awareness for some time, they have only recently found that phonemic awareness in kindergarten is the best predictor of a child's beginning reading success. This means it is a better predictor than IQ or any other measure. In fact, experts have found that a child's level of phonemic awareness upon entering first grade is even more important than the type of reading instruction he or she receives, whether it is whole language or phonics. This is because students must understand that words are made up of sounds, and that these sounds can be manipulated, before they can successfully learn to read. The ability to break words out into individual sounds is crucial to reading and spelling. Once students are capable of doing this they can successfully combine this knowledge with letter-sound correspondence.

It is not surprising that many studies have shown that a phonemic awareness deficit is a principal cause of word identification difficulties. If a student has difficulty hearing and manipulating sounds orally, he or she will have difficulty sounding out words in both reading and writing. Students need direct instruction in phonemic awareness incorporated into their classroom to facilitate their academic success. Early intervention is crucial to their reading acquisition. Most children master phonemic awareness skills by the age of 7; however, gaps in phonemic awareness can still manifest themselves in difficulty with reading and writing. These gaps should be—and can be—addressed at any age.

PHONEMIC AWARENESS AND PHONICS

Many teachers are under the misconception that phonics is simply phonemic awareness renamed. This is not the case. Phonemic awareness is a precursor to phonics instruction, but should not be confused with phonics. Phonics is letter–sound correspondence. It is identifying letters and knowing which letters spell a word. Phonemic awareness is identifying sounds and knowing how many sounds form a word. Phonics is the knowledge that the letters h-a-t spell *hat*, and that the letter *h* makes the /h/ sound; phonemic awareness is the knowledge that there are three sounds in *hat* and then being able to isolate the three sounds. It also reflects the ability to delete /h/ from *hat* to form the word *at*. There is an important reciprocal relationship between letter recognition and phonemic awareness, though, which we will build on during our lessons. There is no reason to teach phonemic awareness in isolation. In fact, experts have found that students learn better when instruction in phonemic awareness and letter recognition are combined.

THE ROLE OF PHONEMIC AWARENESS IN LITERACY ACQUISITION

It is worth injecting a note of caution at this point. Phonemic awareness instruction should by no means replace any other element of reading instruction. It is simply one piece of the puzzle. Literacy skills develop in tandem with the emergence of general cognitive skills and oral language development. This emergence typically begins in the preschool years, depending upon the home environment. A child should have countless experiences with print, whether through listening to a parent or caregiver read a story, looking at a picture book, or staring at the print on a cereal box. Students thus learn to read from left to right, begin at the top of the page, recognize letters, and understand the concept of a word. They also gradually gain a familiarity with story structure if stories are read to them. In addition, a child brings certain necessary cognitive skills to the table. His or her brain must have the capacity to process quickly, which will help the child recognize letters when he or she reads. The child must have a functioning short-term memory so he or she can concentrate on the words in a sentence as he or she reads them, as well as the capacity to retrieve words that are stored in his or her brain. All of these factors influence the successful acquisition of reading and writing skills. Through direct instruction in phonemic awareness we are only addressing one subset of skills, and it is important to keep that in mind while developing your phonemic awareness curriculum.

The understanding of phonemic awareness' place in literacy acquisition can help make instruction more powerful. Studies have shown that the combination of interaction with print and direct instruction in phonemic awareness abilities is the best procedure for developing literacy skills. Preschoolers may be capable of recognizing and generating rhymes, but researchers have shown children are not capable of segmenting and manipulating sounds without some prior reading skill. This makes sense; a child who has had no print exposure will not be able to complete first-grade-level phonemic awareness tasks. Phonemic awareness and reading skills should develop in tandem. After all, alphabet knowledge is necessary for the separation of onsets and rimes, and awareness of onsets and rimes is necessary for decoding. That is why we suggest using letters to represent sounds in our activities as soon as the students can recognize them.

HOW TO USE THIS BOOK

The activities we have presented in this book are meant to be fun and engaging. There is no reason for direct instruction in phonemic awareness to have any tinge of "drill and kill." Use the assessment information in Chapter 1 to decide where you want to begin instruction. Keep in mind that while phonemic awareness skills should be seen as a developmental continuum, there is no strict hierarchy. Some students might master segmenting syllables before learning to generate a rhyme. Do not be concerned by this. It is also okay to move on if a few of your students haven't mastered a certain task. They should continue with repeated practice of the skill but move on to the next level. We have supplied three types of activities in this book. Classroom, literature, and transition activities are provided for young and older children beginning with Chapter 2, although we did not feel the need to create older student activities for listening awareness. Each activity lists the materials needed along with its procedure.

Classroom Activities

These self-explanatory activities can be done with small groups or the entire class. It is also possible to modify them for individual instruction. These activities provide the most direct instruction.

Literature Activities

Research has shown that vocabulary growth plays a significant role in phonemic awareness. As children build their vocabulary, their internal categorization of words builds their phonemic skills. This is one of the many reasons meaningful experiences with literature are so important. We have chosen outstanding literature that either builds phonemic awareness or can be used as a base for phonemic awareness activities.

Transition Time Activities

These are quick activities that can be put to use during classroom line-ups or during a few minutes of free time. It is a great way to keep your students focused on learning while you shift gears in the classroom. Keep in mind that while transition time activities are there for your convenience, it is important to primarily use a combination of classroom-based and literature-based activities with your students.

We hope you enjoy the book—and more important, we hope your students have fun with it too!

ASSESSMENT

The assessment is meant to be used as a pre- and posttest to determine both where to begin instruction with your students and when to move on to the next area of skill instruction. This assessment is best given to students individually. If your students score at different levels of phonemic awareness, you may want to break them into small groups for appropriate instruction.

RHYMING

Do the following words rhyme (if your student is not familiar with the word "rhyme," you can simply ask if the words "sound the same")?

1. Cat-hat   (y)   _____
2. Rock-star   (n)   _____
3. Mop-top   (y)   _____

Pick the rhyming pair:

1. Rope-soar-soap   (rope-soap)   _____
2. Lock-sock-sun   (lock-sock)   _____
3. Foot-fill-hill   (fill-hill)   _____

Tell me a word that rhymes with (nonsense words are acceptable):

1. Car _____
2. Hot _____
3. Bed _____

SENTENCES INTO WORDS

1. How many words do you hear in the sentence "School is fun"? (3) _____
2. How many words do you hear in the sentence "I like milk and cookies"? (5) _____
3. How many words do you hear in the question "Do you know what time it is"? (7) _____
4. How many words are in the sentence "The bear is under the chair"? (6) _____

BEGINNING AND ENDING SOUNDS

1. What is the first sound in the word "boy"? (/b/) _____
2. What is the first sound in the word "happy"? (/h/) _____
3. What is the first sound in the word "chair"? (/ch/) _____
4. What is the last sound in the word "hair"? (/r/) _____
5. What is the last sound in the word "game"? (/m/) _____
6. What is the last sound in the word "desk"? (/k/) _____

BLENDING AND SEGMENTING

Syllables

How many syllables (or word parts, if your students do not know what a syllable is) do you hear in:

1. Sandwich (2) _____

2. Pencil   (2)   _____
3. Soup   (1)   _____
4. Computer   (3)   _____

Phonemes

I'm going to say some sounds and I want you to put them together:

1. C-u-p   (cup)   _____
2. G-a-te   (gate)   _____
3. C-l-o-ck   (clock)   _____
4. How many sounds do you hear in the word "gum"? (3) _____
5. How many sounds do you hear in the word "flame"? (4) _____
6. How many sounds do you hear in the word "shut"? (3) _____

PHONEME MANIPULATION

1. Say "hop" without saying /h/.   (op)   _____
2. Say "goose" without saying /g/. (oose) _____
3. Say "cute" without saying /t/.   (cue)   _____
4. Say "stop" without saying /p/.   (stoh) _____
5. Say "flat" without saying /l/.   (fat)   _____
6. Say "truck" without saying /r/. (tuck) _____
7. Say "gap"—then say it again but instead of saying /g/ say /l/. (lap) _____
8. Say "home"—then say it again but instead of saying /h/ say /f/. (fome) _____
9. Say "tap"—then say it again but instead of saying /a/ say /i/. (tip) _____
10. Say "rug"—then say it again but instead of saying /u/ say /a/. (rag) _____
11. Say "shin"—then say it again but instead of saying /n/ say /p/. (ship) _____
12. Say "grab"—then say it again but instead of saying /b/ say /m/. (gram) _____
13. Say "top"—then add /s/ at the beginning. (stop) _____

14. Say "lip"—then add /f/ at the beginning.   (flip)   ____
15. Say "lug"—then add /p/ at the beginning. (plug)   ____

SCORING

If your students get 50% or less correct in any area tested, then we recommend instruction. If a student does not make progress after considerable time is spent on instruction and practice, we recommend formal testing of the child.

If your students get 50–80% correct, we recommend using the activities in all three sections of the chapter addressing that specific skill.

If your students get 80–85% correct in any area tested, you may just want to do a few transition activities in that particular area.

If your students get 90% or higher correct, there is no need for instruction.

2

LISTENING AWARENESS

Aprerequisite skill for phonemic awareness is the ability to listen. Young children are often inundated by noise, whether it be speech, music, television, or sounds from outside their homes. It is easy to hear these sounds, but a conscious focus on sounds takes some effort. These beginning activities are designed to develop students' listening skills. Once they are able to focus their attention on the sounds they hear, they will be ready to learn phonemic awareness skills.

The activities in this chapter ask students to first recognize what constitutes good listening. They also develop auditory memory and sequencing skills. Once students are able to recognize and *identify* sounds they hear, they are asked to locate sounds. Their analytic skills are called upon as they learn to identify missing sounds in a sound sequence. This will help them in later phoneme analysis exercises. These activities also teach students the importance of paying attention and following directions. This is not only a listening skill but also a crucial skill for children to possess both in our classrooms and in their everyday lives. Listening is a core element of every child's education.

CLASSROOM ACTIVITIES

We Listen With . . .

Materials Needed: chart paper, markers

Begin by titling a chart "We Listen With . . . " Ask your students what parts of their bodies they use to listen. The most obvious response from children is "ears." Write "ears" on the chart or draw ears for nonreaders. Explain to the children that we hear with other parts of our bodies. For example, we use our eyes to look at the speaker. Ask the children "What if Elizabeth (a classmate) is speaking? That's right, we should be looking at Elizabeth." Continue by explaining that we use our mouths to listen by keeping them closed when someone else is speaking. We also use our brain. It stores what we hear, sorts it, and then tells our body what to do with that information. Finally, explain that we use our hands and feet—by keeping them still.

Marco Polo

Materials Needed: ears and a blindfold

Choose one child to be Marco and blindfold him. The child should call out "Marco." Point to another child and have that child call out "Polo." The child who is blindfolded must listen carefully to the voice and try to identify who said "Polo." If this proves too difficult, try the variation below.

Variation: Play the game the same way, but have the blindfolded child identify the area from which the voice came.

Who's on First?

Materials Needed: the "We Listen With . . . " chart, ears, various objects around the room

Begin this activity by explaining that sounds are everywhere. Have the children close their eyes for a few minutes and listen to the sounds around them. Prompt them for outdoor sounds and even sounds from within themselves. Ask the students to name the different sounds they hear.

In the second part of this activity, choose one child to cover his eyes and three other children to sit in spots designated as first, second, and third base. The children on each base take a turn making a familiar noise, such as dropping a block, coughing, or shaking keys. The blindfolded child must answer the questions "Who's on first?" "Who's on second? "Who's on third?" The child must respond in sequence, saying "Someone is shaking keys on first base, someone is coughing on second base, and someone dropped a block on third base." Encourage the students to speak in complete sentences. You may want to begin this activity with one or two bases and progress to three when you feel your students are ready.

Which Sound Is Missing?

Materials Needed: various objects around the room

Instruct the students to close their eyes. While their eyes are closed, you should make a series of sounds such as those mentioned above or new ones, such as crumpling paper and turning a book's pages. Repeat the sequence of sounds, but omit one sound. The children must identify which sound is missing.

Follow My Directions

Materials Needed: none

Give a child a set of directions. It is important that the students follow the directions in the order in which they are presented. Begin with 2- or 3-step directions and gradually increase the number of steps as the children develop mastery of the skill.

Examples:

Take out your pencil and paper.
Get up from your seat and push in your chair.

Stand up, walk to the door, knock three times.

Stand up, walk to the board, write your name.

Touch your head, touch your nose, touch your shoulders, fold your hands.

Stand up, push in your chair, walk to the closet, open the door, take out your coat, go back to your seat, sit down.

Simon Sez

Materials Needed: none

Students play this familiar game, which hones their listening skills. Children have to listen to be sure that "Simon Sez" was indeed said before making a move. A child is only allowed to move if the direction is preceded by the words "Simon Sez."

If Simon does not say "Simon Sez" before a movement and the child follows the move then he or she must sit down.

LITERATURE-BASED ACTIVITIES

The use of various nursery rhymes, children's poems, and finger plays are all excellent resources to playfully introduce and expose children to the sounds of language.

Rain, Rain Go Away

Materials Needed: none

On a rainy day, sing the nursery rhyme "Rain, Rain Go Away":

Rain, rain go away,

Come back another day.

All the children want to play

So rain, rain go away.

One, Two, Buckle My Shoe

Materials Needed: numbers 1–10 written in large print on large-size pieces of cardstock (one number per card).

After introducing numbers to your students, teach this little poem. Distribute the numbered cards to the children. They must step forward and hold up their number card when they hear their number recited in the poem.

1, 2 buckle my shoe
3, 4 open the door
5, 6 pick up sticks
7, 8 lay them straight
9, 10 let's start all over again

TRANSITION ACTIVITIES

Use these activities as you move from one activity to another.

Whoooo's Listening?

Materials Needed: none

To get the children's attention when transitioning from one activity to another, try these simple directions:

If you're listening, your hands are on your shoulders.
If you're listening, your hands are on your head.
If you're listening, your hands are on your hips.
If you're listening, your hands are folded in your lap.

Our Morning Song

Materials Needed: none

Sing this song with your students every morning to get them ready to start the day.

Let's come together and start our day.
Let's come together and start our day.
Let's come together and start our day,
And listen to what we have to say.

The Listening Song

Materials Needed: none

This is a song to ensure that your students are listening to you. Sing it to the tune of "If You're Happy and You Know It."

If you're listening and you know it, clap your hands.
If you're listening and you know it, stamp your feet.
If you're listening and you know it, and you really want to show it,
If your listening and you know it, fold your hands.

What's My Pattern?

Materials Needed: hands, feet

This activity is a good way to draw children together or to gain their attention for an important announcement. Make a pattern of sounds, such as clapping your hands twice or stomping your feet three times. Children must repeat the pattern they hear.

RHYME
AND ALLITERATION

R hyming is the beginning level of phonemic awareness, and one that is often the focus of the literature and play of early childhood. Nursery rhymes, Dr. Seuss, and playground games such as "Miss Mary Mack" develop children's ability to recognize and generate rhymes. Parents and teachers may be unaware of the benefits they provide children through reading nursery rhymes, but in actuality this lays a foundation for phonemic awareness. A clear relationship exists between knowledge of nursery rhymes and early reading skills. Young children hear words that sound the same and develop an appreciation for rhymes. Experts have found that rhyme play draws children's attention to the notion that language has not only meaning and message but form as well. Furthermore, children begin to understand that not only do words have form, many actually share the same form.

Many researchers suggest that very young children and older children who have little sensitivity to the sound structure of language should first focus on rhyme. Use the results of your assessment to determine if this is an appropriate starting point for your students. If older students have difficulty reading through analogy (word patterns), it would also be a good idea to develop their rhyming skills. Once children can hear rhymes they can intuitively recognize that the onset (the first consonant[s] in a word preceding the first vowel) is exchanged for another phoneme in word patterns.

The activities in this chapter are geared toward discovering that words have form in addition to meaning and message. We have placed the activities in this chapter in order of difficulty. Students first learn to be aware of rhyme through example. Once children are able to recognize rhyme, instruction should focus on the students' ability to generate rhymes through literature and games. They are then asked to discriminate rhyming and nonrhyming words. Finally, we ask them to generate their own rhymes.

Alliteration taps into the same skill as rhyming for students, noting the similarities in words. Young children, therefore, often find tongue twisters as enjoyable as rhymes. Alliteration activities are intentionally listed after classroom rhyming activities in this chapter. It is recommended that you wait for your students to show mastery in rhyme production before incorporating alliteration into your phonemic awareness activities. Researchers report that without a clear understanding of rhyme, children are apt to confuse the concept of words beginning with the same sound (the onset) with the concept of rhyme. For example, in our experience we have found that many kindergartners often think "bat" and "ball" rhyme because they share initial sounds.

A NOTE ON OLDER STUDENTS

If older students are having difficulty identifying and producing rhymes, they might simply be lacking in exposure to rhymes. Students from backgrounds that are not literacy rich may not have had experience with rhyming books as young children. Another possibility is that they simply do not understand what is being asked of them. Repeated exposure to rhymes and explicit directions are the key to instruction.

CLASSROOM ACTIVITIES

You're Out!

Materials Needed: rhyming picture cards

To ensure that your students can discriminate between words that do and do not rhyme, try playing "You're Out!" In this game, the students get to pretend they are umpires in a baseball game. Show the children three pictures, two that rhyme and one that does not. Have children identify the picture in the group that doesn't rhyme with the other two pictures. The children throw it out in a little garbage bag or can and say, "You're out!!!!"

Which One of These Is Not Like the Other? (Older Student Activity)

Materials Needed: none

This is similar to "You're Out!" but it is geared toward older students. The students are orally given a group of three words and are asked to pick out the word that does not rhyme with the other two. For example: clock/mop/stock, mouse/dice/house, hit/hat/bat, spin/bin/ban. You should start with easy examples, such as high/fly/shoelace, and then make it more difficult (lint/mint/bin) after the students have had some success with the activity.

Same or Different? (Older Student Activity)

Materials Needed: none

This is another discrimination activity for older students to hone their rhyming skills. The teacher begins by saying, "Chair, hair. Same or different?"

The student responds "same." The conversation might proceed as follows:

Teacher: "Good! What about shoelace/sneaker?"
Student: "Different."

Who Has a Rhyming Word?

Materials Needed: rhyming picture cards

Distribute one picture from a pair of rhyming pictures to each child. Hold up a picture and ask, "Who has a picture that rhymes with *frog*?" The child with the rhyming picture should hold up his or her picture for all to see. Say, "Michael has a picture that rhymes with frog." Then ask, "Does *log* rhyme with *frog*?" Have children respond yes or no. Do the same for the rest of the pictures.

Find the Rhyme

Materials Needed: rhyming picture pairs

Begin by introducing various pictures of rhyming words by name. Attach the pictures to a felt-board or chalkboard. Choose one picture and have children find the matching rhyming picture. Place it next to the first picture. The teacher says each word aloud and the students echo. The students must then determine if the two words rhyme.

Find the Rhyme by Sight (Older Student Activity)

Materials Needed: poem or song lyrics

In this activity, older students are asked to pay attention to the way words look to determine if they rhyme. Since your older students are presumably reading, they can use their eyes to help them determine what rhymes. Write a poem or song on the board and read it aloud to the students. Ask a student to point out the rhyming word pairs. In this activity, it would be best to use rhyming words that have the same word pattern. For example, *feet* and *meat* rhyme, but their different spellings might confuse your students.

Clip It!

Materials Needed: rhyming picture cards and clothespins

This activity can be used in a phonemic awareness center or as an independent activity. Using various rhyming picture cards, have the children find two to four pictures that rhyme. They then use a clothespin to clip the pictures together.

Find Your Rhyming Partner

Materials Needed: rhyming picture cards

Distribute one rhyming picture card to each child. Ensure that there is an even amount so that every child will have a rhyme partner. Initially, you may want to have one child at a time walk around to find their rhyme partner. As they become familiar with rhyming, all the children can walk around at the same time to find the classmate that has a picture that rhymes with their picture. Once they find their rhyming partner they sit down next to each other. Have each pair of children say their words aloud and ask the rest of the class whether or not they truly are rhyme partners.

Heads and Feet

Materials Needed: none

In this activity drawn from Patricia Cunningham,[1] children play a game in which they point to words that rhyme with their *heads* and *feet*. After you say each word, the students decide if the word rhymes with *head* or *feet*. Once they decide they point to their heads or their feet. You might want to use some of the following words:

treat	bread	led	sleet
seat	red	sheet	fed
bed	beat	sled	thread
dead	greet	heat	shed

Now, ask the students to say the missing word in the following riddles (for *head*):

On a sandwich, we put something in between the . . .
Goldilocks fell asleep in Baby Bear's . . .
To sew, you need a needle and . . .
Rudolph the Reindeer's nose is . . .
We can ride down snowy hills on a . . .

Here are other riddles, the answers to which rhyme with *feet*:

On Halloween you might say Trick or . . .
When you come into class the teacher asks you to take your . . .
You make your bed with a . . .
When you are cold, you turn on the . . .

You can also do this activity with the words *hand* and *knee*.

Create a Rhyme Book

Materials Needed: writing tools and paper

Each child should make up a rhyming pair that you will write. Have the children illustrate each word. You may collect the pages and publish them as a class book, or have children make up additional rhyming pairs to assemble and publish individual rhyming books to keep. They can add them to their own personal book collections.

Sing a Song: Roll a Ball

Materials Needed: ball

Have the children sit in a circle on the floor to play this game. Sung to the tune of "Row, Row, Row Your Boat":

Roll, roll, roll our ball
Gently to a friend. Give us a word that sounds like _____ (the child that is rolling the ball looks around the room and picks a word)
Then we'll roll again (the child who receives the ball must provide a rhyming word before rolling the ball again. Nonsense words are acceptable).

Song Lyrics for Older Students

Materials Needed: song lyrics and highlighters

Students in middle and high school will generally not want to sing songs geared toward young children. Instead, it is always a good idea to tap into your students' interests. Their favorite singers undoubtedly employ rhymes in their music. Play the students' favorite songs for them and ask them to find the words that sound the same. Write the lyrics down and read them slowly to your student. Help him or her pick out the rhymes. Practice this until the student can complete the task independently.

Song Books for Older Students

Materials Needed: song lyrics by popular musicians or students

This is similar to the rhyme book for younger students. Instead of cutting out pictures of rhymes, students can collect rhyming stanzas from their favorite songs. They can thus create their own rhyme book using songs from their favorite artists. Students can be encouraged to create their own raps/songs that rhyme to include in their book.

Rhyming and Riddles for Older Students

Materials Needed: none

If students are still having difficulty with rhymes, try using some of these riddles with them. Read each sentence to them, emphasizing the italic word. This word must be replaced with a rhyming word in order for the sentence to make sense.

I was late for work today because my car wouldn't *smart*.
I went to the movies last night but couldn't get in because the 10 o'clock was sold *kraut*.
It's a tie game and the bases are *goaded*.
My sister screamed last night because she saw a *louse*.
If you eat too much candy your teeth will start to *pot*.
They say that if you drink too much caffeine it will stunt your *both*.
Around election time there are a lot of ads saying "don't forget to *moat!*"

Once the students are adept at supplying the correct answer, ask them to create their own riddles for you or another student to solve.

Alliteration and Students' Names

Materials Needed: writing tools and paper

Cunningham[2] suggests this idea for teaching alliteration. After reading tongue twister books to your students, you can create a tongue twister book for your class using their names. Here are some ideas:

Billy's **b**aby **b**rother **b**opped **B**etty.
Carol **c**an **c**atch **c**aterpillars.

Hungry **H**arry **h**ates **h**amburgers.
Gorgeous **G**abrielle **g**ets **g**ood **g**rades.

Alphabet Alliteration

Materials Needed: none

Beginning with the letter *a*, children go through the letters of the alphabet to make up alliteration tongue twisters. They add a girl's name, a boy's name, an object, and a place that begin with the target letter into the sing-song example below. Once children are familiar with this activity they can hop on one foot or jump on two feet each time they say a word that begins with the target letter.

A my name is **A**nnie, my husband's name is **A**l; we come from **A**labama, just to sell **a**pples.

Who Knows My Rule? Alliteration

Materials Needed: object tubs or pictures

Explain to the children that they are going to play a game called "Who Knows My Rule?" All of the objects/pictures that the instructor shows them are going to follow a special rule. The students should name the objects with the teacher. For example, you might begin by showing them pictures of a bat, bee, bug, bird, and a ball. Ask the children, "Who knows my rule?" The children should notice that all the objects/pictures begin with the same sound. The rule is, therefore, that they must start with the letter *b*.

Variation: Play this game with your students orally instead of with pictures or objects. Present a sentence to your students after explaining that all of the words in the sentence follow a special rule. Before beginning, prompt your students to listen very carefully!

LITERATURE-BASED ACTIVITIES

There are numerous rhyming books that can be used for the activities below (see Appendix C). Here are just a few examples of how rhyming books can be used for rhyme instruction.

The Hungry Thing

Materials Needed: *The Hungry Thing* by Jan Slepian and Ann Seidler,[3] pictures of food or plastic toy food, a paper version of the Hungry Thing with a cut out mouth.

Before reading this story, tell the children, "I want you to listen very carefully to some of the foods the Hungry Thing wants to eat. See if you notice anything about these foods." During the reading, encourage the children to name the real food with you as you read it aloud. After the reading, ask the children to identify pictures of food. Tell them you are going to pretend to be the Hungry Thing and will say the name of the food you would like to eat just as the Hungry Thing would. Hang the paper version of the Hungry Thing around your neck and begin by saying "Feed me!" The class asks, "What would you like to eat?" Respond as Hungry Thing by using nonsense words that rhyme with the pictures of food they previously identified. For example, "beans" would be "feans." If the two words rhyme the child is rewarded by "feeding" the Hungry Thing and becoming its friend.

Variation: Have the children become "The Hungry Child." Spread out pictures of various food items (or play/plastic food). One child silently chooses an item. That child then says, "Feed me!" The rest of the class says, "What would you like to eat?" The Hungry Child says the name of the food the way the Hungry Thing would say it (using a nonsense word that rhymes with the real word). Once the rest of the class knows what the "Hungry Child" wants to eat, choose one child to give the food's proper name and give its picture to the "Hungry Child."

"Sick" and "Jimmy Jet and His TV Set"

Materials Needed: *Where the Sidewalk Ends* by Shel Silverstein[4]

Older students are likely to be resistant to reading Dr. Seuss or other rhyming books geared toward small children because they will find them "too babyish." Shel Silverstein is a wonderful alternative. *Where the Sidewalk Ends* (1974) is an excellent resource for rhymes older students will enjoy.

Begin by reading the poem "Sick" to your students. After reading the entire poem, discuss it with your students. What did they notice about each line? Did they hear the rhymes? Read it to them again. If necessary, point out that two lines end with the same sound: *today/McKay, mumps/bumps, dry/eye*, and so forth. Once this has been established, try the same procedure using a poem with alternating rhyming lines, such as "Jimmy Jet and His TV Set." Ask your student to identify the rhyming pairs in the stanza. Can they think of another word that rhymes with *set*? *You*?

There's a Wocket in My Pocket

Materials Needed: *There's a Wocket in My Pocket* by Dr. Seuss and a cut-out of a creature from the story

Read the book to your students. After reading the book ask your students if they noticed anything about the words in the story. Did they notice that they all rhymed? Using the cut-out creature, pass it around the room by putting the creature on a different article of clothing, such as buttons on a shirt, a hood on a jacket, a zipper, or a shoelace. Have the child make up a nonsense word that rhymes with that article of clothing, saying, "There's a *mutton* on my *button*" or "There's a *tood* on my *hood*."

TRANSITION TIME ACTIVITIES

Use these activities to transition from one activity to another.

The Name Game

Materials Needed: none

This activity can be used when calling children to pack up at the end of the day or before gathering their belongings for lunch. Each child must produce a word that rhymes with his or her name before leaving his or her seat and gathering belongings. No child should be left in his or her seat because the child was unable to produce a rhyme. Ask the child if he or she would like some help from a friend, and then provide the child with another opportunity to make a rhyme.

Variation: You might provide a word that does or does not rhyme with a child's name. That child must respond yes or no to signify if it rhymes. Or explain to the children that you're going to call them one at a time to get ready for dismissal. Instead of calling them by their names, you are going to call them by a silly name, one that sounds like (or rhymes with) their name. Say a word that rhymes with a child's name without identifying the child. The children must listen for the words that sound like their names.

Thumbs Up, Thumbs Down

Materials Needed: none

In this activity, have the children listen as you say two words. If the words rhyme or sound alike, the children must put their thumbs up. If the words do not rhyme or sound alike, then the children must put their thumbs down.

NOTES

1. From Patricia Cunningham, *Phonics They Use* © 2000. Published by Allyn & Bacon, Boston, MA. Copyright © 2000 by Pearson Education. Adapted by permission of the publisher.

2. From Patricia Cunningham, *Phonics They Use* © 2000.

3. J. Slepian & A. Seidler. (2001). *The Hungry Thing*. Chicago: Follett.

4. S. Silverstein. (1974). *Where the Sidewalk Ends: Poems and Drawings*. New York: Harper & Row.

SENTENCES TO WORDS

As young children become more aware of their surroundings, they also begin to recognize print. They see it on the back of their cereal boxes and in the McDonald's sign they pass on the way home from school. Many children come to school ready for literacy acquisition because they have had many experiences with the written word. They have a clear understanding that we speak and read words, and have a general understanding of the relation between speech and print. Other students, however, come to school without having had any print exposure. These children require direct instruction in separating sentences into words. Speech is an innate skill, but understanding that sentences are made up of words is not.

Separating sentences into words is an easy and fun skill to teach your students. Therefore, be sure your students have mastered this before beginning literacy instruction. In addition, the activities in this chapter will not only help students understand that sentences are made up of words, but will also reinforce print directionality. These are important steps on the road to beginning reading.

CLASSROOM ACTIVITIES

Count the Words

Materials Needed: counters such as cubes, beads, buttons or edible counters such as raisins, M&Ms, Cheerios, plus a cup

Begin by telling the students that sentences are made up of individual words. Write two sentences on the board and ask the students to compare them. They should determine which sentence is longer and then count the words together. How many more words are in the longer sentence? Explain that some sentences may have a few words, while others may have more words. The next activity involves using M&Ms to represent words. Pick a sentence from a familiar read-aloud story. Say the sentence, and then repeat it again slowly while placing one M&M in the cup for every word. The class counts the M&Ms together to learn how many words were in the sentence.[1]

Pass the Potato

Materials Needed: a plastic potato or a real one

In this game, the teacher makes up a sentence about one of the children while the children are seated in a circle. If you choose "Jonathan is wearing brown boots," say it once and have the students repeat it in unison. Then, the first child says the first word in the sentence and then passes the potato to the child next to him or her, who says the next word, and so forth. The potato is passed among the children until the sentence is completed. The next child takes the potato, a sentence is created about him or her, and the game continues.

Cut-Up Sentences

Materials Needed: sentence strips, marker

Pick a sentence from a book familiar to the children or ask a child to dictate his or her own sentence to you. Let the students watch you write the sentence on a sentence strip as you segment the words aloud. Cut up the sentence word by word in front of the students. Mix up the words from this sentence and have students reassemble the sentence in a pocket chart.

Sentence Builders

Materials Needed: sentence strips, markers

The first step is to create a "Things I Like" chart. Each student tells you "I like to . . ." and you write the sentence followed by his or her name on a chart. Next, let the children in your class be the words. Write each word on a sentence strip and then cut it up. Distribute the words to students and have them line up in front of the class with the words in the proper sentence order. Repeat this with other sentences from the chart, letting the students gain some independence in building the sentences.[2]

Heads and Shoulders

Materials Needed: none

You might want to begin this activity with a short sentence, like "My name is Christopher." Have the students touch their heads for the word "my," their shoulders for the word "name," their heads for the word "is," and their shoulders for their name. Continue on with new sentences that increase in length.

Hopping on Words

Materials Needed: roll of large paper

On large sheet of paper, write out a sentence with plenty of space between the words. Have one student hop onto each word as the class chants the sentence in unison. The child hopping has to make sure he or she is hopping on a word as the class simultaneously chants that word. Then the next child takes a turn. It's a good idea to provide a new sentence after a few students have had a turn.

Word Jump

Materials Needed: construction paper

Choose a sentence and write each word on separate pieces of construction paper. Be sure to include a piece of paper for the period, since awareness of punctuation must be reinforced. Mix up the words so that they are not in sentence order and lay them closely together on the floor. Let's say you chose the sentence "Today is Monday." One student will find the word "Today" first and jump on it. He or she will then jump to the second and third words in the sentence, and finally the period.

Invented Spelling

Materials Needed: pencil and paper

When the students are writing independently, try this activity to help them separate sentences into words. Once they have decided what sentence they want to write, have them count how many words are in the sentence on their fingertips. The space between their fingers represents the space between the words, so when they're writing they will remember to use proper spacing. This is a good way for them to check their work too, by counting the space between their fingers to see if it corresponds with the number of spaces on their papers.

LITERATURE-BASED ACTIVITIES

Caps for Sale

Materials Needed: *Caps for Sale* by Esphyr Slobodkina,[3] sentence strips, stapler

After reading *Caps for Sale*, choose a sentence from the story and write one word from the sentence on each strip. Then make caps for the children by rounding the sentence strips and stapling the ends together. Each child must be the word by putting a cap on his or her head, and then stand in sentence order.

Pop Up

Materials Needed: nursery rhymes or poems

This activity is similar to "Pass the Potato." Say a sentence aloud or use a familiar nursery rhyme that the children can recite from memory. Start with one student, who pops out of his or her chair when you say the first word. The student on his or her right pops out of his or her chair upon hearing the second word, and it continues down the line of students until the end of the sentence.

Space Awareness

Materials Needed: big books

During story time, ask the students to count how many spaces they see in a sentence. Explain that those spaces separate the words, and that's how you know you're seeing the next word in a sentence.

TRANSITION ACTIVITIES

Use these activities to move from one activity to another or to end your day.

Word Count

Materials Needed: none

Read aloud a sentence from a familiar storybook or make up one of your own. Use the children's names to gain their attention and motivation. Ask children to listen to the sentence and count the number of words in the sentence. When they have the correct number, the children should hold up that many fingers. As you look around the room, choose children with the correct number to line up or transition to the next activity or area of the room.

Variation: You might also want to do this as a warm-up for math by having the children write the number on a slate or dry erase board once they have learned to write numbers.

Pop-Up Home

Materials Needed: none

When it is the end of the day, say "Line up." The student closest to you will pop up and say "line," and the student next to him or her will pop up and say the word "up." They will get their coats as you say the sentence "Go get your coats." The next four students will repeat the steps, popping up for each word in the sentence.

CHAPTER 4

NOTES

1. From Patricia Cunningham, *Phonics They Use* © 2000. Published by Allyn & Bacon, Boston. Copyright © 2000 by Pearson Education. Adapted by permission of the publisher.

2. From Patricia Cunningham, *Phonics They Use* © 2000.

3. E. Slobodkina. (1987). *Caps for Sale*. New York: Harper Trophy.

BEGINNING AND ENDING SOUNDS

As children become adept at identifying and categorizing sounds through rhyme and alliteration, they are ready to move on to isolating beginning and ending sounds in words. Experts report that learning to isolate the initial phoneme in a word is the first step in phoneme segmentation. This is sometimes a difficult skill to master and will take your students time to learn. During instruction, it is important to remember that some exercises in phonemic awareness are more conducive to learning than others. Researchers note that while teaching beginning and ending sound identification, phonemes' individual characteristics are easier to feel during articulation than they are to hear while being spoken by another. Therefore, help your students focus on articulation. Draw your students' attention to the shape of their mouths and location of their tongues when they are producing a sound. This will help them internalize the sounds.

While using the activities in this chapter, bear in mind that it is much easier to identify the beginning sound in a word than it is to identify the final sound. Spend as much time as needed on the beginning sounds in words before you move on to the more difficult final sound. Say the words slowly for your students, and take your time enunciating the sounds at the beginning and end of each word.

With the exception of the "Crossword Puzzle" game, activities in this chapter can be used for either beginning or ending sounds. While students are identifying phonemes, make sure they are in fact telling you the sound, not letter, that a word begins with. We blend sounds together, not letter names together. Remember, these activities are about phonemic awareness, not phonics knowledge.

CLASSROOM ACTIVITIES

Find Your Beginning or Ending Sound Partner

Materials Needed: picture cards

This activity is played just like "Find Your Rhyming Partner." Distribute one picture card to each child. Remember there should be an even amount so that every child will have a beginning sound partner. If you have an odd number of students, you can be a sound partner too. Have the children walk around to find the classmate who has a picture that begins with the same sound as their picture. Once they find their beginning sound partner the pair should sit down next to each other. Have each pair of children say their words aloud and ask the rest of the class if they are beginning sound partners. "Find Your Ending Sound Partner" is played the same way. Initially, you may want to have one child at a time walk around to find his or her ending sound partner because ending sounds are a bit more difficult for children to identify.

Scavenger Sound Hunt

Materials Needed: *Where's Waldo?* or *I Spy* books

Using a *Where's Waldo?* or *I Spy* book, ask the children if they can find something in the picture that begins with the /s/ sound. As the children learn new sounds in class, you should incorporate these into the game. When the children are ready, have them locate various pictures that end, rather than begin, with a particular sound. This type of game can be played anywhere, whether on a field trip, in the classroom, the supermarket, or around the kitchen. Ask the child if he or she can find something in the kitchen that begins with the /p/ sound. Possible words could be pot, plate, pan, pasta, potato, and so forth.

On Your Mark, Get Set, Draw (or Write)

Materials Needed: marker, crayon or pencil, paper

The children will listen to you say, "On your mark, get ready, get set, draw . . . a picture that begins with the /b/ sound, GO." Children can draw any picture that begins with that sound. If they can't think of a word themselves, tell them to look around the room for help. Continue to play this game using other sounds. If your students are ready, this game can also be played by having children write a word that begins with a particular sound. Invented spelling is acceptable for this activity.

I'm Going on a Picnic

Materials Needed: none

Invite the students on a pretend picnic. They can only come on the imaginary picnic if they bring something that begins with the last sound in their name. Nicole can bring lemonade and Katelinn can bring napkins. Have the children sit in a circle and say, "I'm going on a picnic and I'm going to bring . . ." The other students decide if they have chosen an item that begins with the correct sound.

You're Out

Materials Needed: matching sound picture cards

This activity is also used in Chapter 3. To ensure that your students can discriminate between words that do and do not have the same beginning and ending sound, try playing "You're Out!" In this game, the students get to pretend they are umpires in a baseball game. Show the children three pictures, two that have the same initial sound and one that does not. Have children identify the picture in the group that doesn't start with the same sound as the other two pictures. The children throw it out in a little garbage bag or can and say, "You're out!!!!"

Sound of the Day

Materials Needed: none

Choose a sound each morning and tell your students that it will be the sound of the day. Tell the students that the object of the activity is to see how many words they can come up with by 3 o'clock (or the end of the school day). The students should listen for words that begin or end with that sound throughout the day. Keep a list of all the words the students found.

Start and Finish

Materials Needed: a little start and finish race flag

Tell your students that each word is in a race. Say a word for the students, such as *game*. Ask the students where the /m/ sound is—at the start of the race or the end of the race, which is represented by the finish line.

Read My Mind

Materials Needed: none

Explain to the children that you have something on your mind from their spelling or vocabulary words of the week. Tell them that you are only going to tell them the beginning sound of the object you have in mind. If after several tries they haven't guessed what it is, then tell them the ending sound of the thing of which you're thinking. If the word is *pencil* say, "I'm thinking of something that begins with the /p/ sound." If they're unable to guess the word say, "This word ends with the /l/ sound."

Word Box

Materials Needed: picture cards and index card box

Place all of the picture cards you have in a box. Each child chooses one card out of the box. They must tell you the beginning and ending sound of the picture they see.

Variation for Older Students: If the students know their letters, they should give both the letter and the letter sound for the beginning and ending sounds.

Crossword Puzzle (Older Student Activity)

Materials Needed: chalkboard or large wipe-off board

Pick a topic for your crossword puzzle such as animals. Additional topics could be food, names, or games. Ask the children to name an animal that begins with the /k/ sound, like cat. Write it on the board. Now have children tell you the last sound they hear in cat. When you have the right answer, say "That's right, /t/ is the last sound in cat." Now have the children think of an animal that begins with the /t/ sound, like tiger. Write tiger vertically using the "t" in "cat" as the first letter. Now have children identify the last sound in tiger as /r/. Ask the children who can think of an animal that begins with the sound /r/, such as rabbit. Your crossword puzzle should look like this:

$$\textbf{c a t}$$
$$\textbf{i}$$
$$\textbf{g}$$
$$\textbf{e}$$
$$\textbf{r a b b i t}$$

LITERATURE-BASED ACTIVITIES

Tongue Twisters

Materials Needed: a variety of tongue twisters

Read a tongue twister to the children. Ask the children to listen for the "popular" sound, or the sound they hear the most, at the beginning of the words. Have children identify that sound.

Ms. Beginning, Mr. End

Materials Needed: any storybook

Read a familiar storybook to the children. At the end of the story reread the last sentence. Break the children into pairs. One child will be "Mr. (or Ms.) Beginning," and the other child will be "Mr. (or Ms.) End." Mr. Beginning must identify the beginning sound in the word and tell Mr. End what it is, and Mr.

End must identify the ending sound in the word and tell Mr. Beginning what it is. Then they should switch titles for the next word and try the other task.

Prereading Activity

Materials Needed: storybook

Before reading any book, read the title of the story aloud. Have the children identify the beginning sound of each word in the title. Then have the children identify the ending sound in each word of the title. Repeat this activity using the author's name.

TRANSITION ACTIVITIES

Use these activities to move from one activity to another.

Listen for Your Sound

Materials Needed: none

During transition times, call children to line up or meet on a rug by having them listen for the beginning or ending sound in their name. Say, "If your name begins with the /m/ sound, please line up" or "If your name ends with the /d/ sound please meet me at the rug."

Same Sound

Materials Needed: none

Before students can transition from one activity to the next, they must tell you a word that begins or ends with the beginning or ending sound of their name.

Variation: The students can choose a friend's name for this task. If they choose a friend, the person whose name they used gets the next turn.

BLENDING
AND SEGMENTATION

By the end of kindergarten, most students have mastered the ability to identify beginning and ending sounds. The next step is learning to blend and segment. We automatically blend sounds together to form words when we speak, overlapping phonemes to produce meaningful speech. Toddlers learn to do this, yet these skills are also crucially linked to early reading and spelling skills. When a child successfully sounds out a printed word, he or she is blending the sounds together.

The same holds true for spelling. Successful spelling begins with segmenting and isolating sounds. Reading and writing are a guessing game without the combination of blending and segmenting. It should be noted that segmenting is more challenging than blending, since the students are being asked to produce individual sounds by themselves rather than simply recognizing and articulating them. Although blending and segmenting differ in their levels of difficulty, the skills develop in tandem. We have therefore linked blending and segmenting activities together in this chapter.

Activities in this chapter progress in order of difficulty, as it is easier to blend and segment large chunks of sounds, such as syllables and rimes, than it is to blend smaller units. Syllables are addressed first, followed by onsets and rimes, and then phonemes. In order to be able to blend and split syllables, researchers point out that students must understand that words can be divided into small, meaningless sounds. Begin with compound and/or two-syllable words. Students are generally able to master syllables relatively quickly and are then ready for onsets and rimes. As discussed previously, onsets are the consonants that precede the first vowel in a word. Rimes are the first vowel in a word and all the letters that come after it. For example, in the word *train*, /tr/ is the onset and /ain/ is the rime. In the word *game*, /g/ is the onset and /ame/ is the rime. It is important to remember that alphabet knowledge is a prerequisite for working with onsets and rimes, so don't begin work with these until your students know their letters. Phonemes are the smallest units of sound in the speech stream, and the most difficult to blend and segment. Phonemic segmentation in particular is considered an excellent predictor of early reading and spelling skills. You may want to spend extra time with this section of the chapter. Remember to keep in mind that there is a reciprocal relationship between blending and segmenting skills and reading. The more students practice reading, the more their ability to blend and segment will develop. A final note on this chapter is that while we have ordered the activities by difficulty from syllables through phonemes, each activity can be used for syllables, onsets and rimes, and phonemes.

CLASSROOM ACTIVITIES

Who Knows What I See?

Materials Needed: pictures, small toy objects, or classroom items

This activity is similar to the popular children's game "I Spy." If you are using classroom objects, tell the children that you are going to pick an object in the classroom. You will explain to the children that you are going to say the name of this object in a very silly way as if you're talking in s-l-o-w m-o-t-i-o-n, segmenting it into parts. Segment the word either by syllables, onsets and rimes, or phonemes. Then you can ask, "Who knows what I see?" You can also play this game with a bag of small toys. Choose a toy and segment its name without showing the students the toy. The child who knows what you see gets to hold the object (you may want to buy inexpensive party favor toys that the children can keep). Some possible words are below:

By syllables:	By onset/rime:	By phonemes:
cal/en/dar	cl-ock	d-e-s-k

win/dow	bl-ock	l-igh-t
note/book	ch-air	b-a-s-k-e-t
com/pu/ter	sh-ade	r-u-g
fol/der	br-ush	b-oo-k-s
cray/on	ch-art	p-a-p-er

At the end of this activity, you can expand it and turn it into a segmenting activity. Ask the children if they can say their object in the same silly way that you did. They should segment the word into parts; then you will blend it together using the parts they said. Then ask them if you have put the word back together correctly.

I Spy (Older Student Activity)

Materials Needed: magazines

If you are working with older students, trying using pictures from a magazine for this activity. For example, if you are looking at a picture of the interior of a car, say "dash-board" or "wind-shield." Again, it is important to begin with compound words; then increase the difficulty with multisyllabic words, onsets and rimes, and then individual phonemes. Eventually, you will take the pictures away, and have the students blend the sounds of words you speak. This can then be turned into a segmenting activity, in which the students speak a word in its parts, and you guess what the word is by blending the parts together.

The Memory Game

Materials Needed: two sets of different color cards, one for onsets and one for rimes. (This game can be stored in a resealable plastic bag and put in a word study center for the children to play with during center time.)

This game is played like the traditional memory game. All cards should be set face down. The first player chooses one onset card and one rime card. The player must try to blend the onset and rime to make a word. If he or she is able to blend the word, that player keeps the cards and takes another turn. If the player is unable to blend the onset and rime, he or she must turn the cards face down and the next player takes a turn.

Word Buddies

Materials Needed: syllable cards (see Appendix B for syllable lists)

This game is similar to the "Memory Game." Students are given index cards with syllables written on them. The students have to find a word buddy in their classroom. Their word buddy has a syllable card that can attach to their card to form a real word. Once all of the children find a word buddy, they should try again with the same card to see if they can make a new word buddy.

Word Teams

Materials Needed: chart paper or blackboard

Put a series of five or six letters on the board. Students can work in groups to blend the letters together into words. Allow them 5 to 10 minutes to list all the words they can think of and then write them on the board. If possible, the words should then be divided into word patterns on the board.

Magnetic Letters

Materials Needed: magnetic letters

Magnetic letters are a popular teaching tool ideal for demonstrating blending through manipulatives. They can teach word families once children know letter sounds. The teacher can form a word pattern, such as *–at*, and then ask the students to attach different letters or letter combinations to *–at* in order to make a word. Students should say the sounds of both the onset and rime and then blend them together to say the complete word. Once students have mastered this with word patterns, they can try it with individual phonemes.

Multisensory Blending

Materials Needed: none

In this Orton-Gillingham based activity, demonstrated by Esther Morgan Sands at a professional development workshop for the Reading Reform Foundation of NYC in February 2002, students blend sounds by using their upper bodies. Demonstrate the following for your students: Tap your right shoulder with your left hand while saying /c/. Then tap your left shoulder with the same hand and say /a/. Next, tap the middle of your chest with the same hand and say /ca/. You have just demonstrated multisensory blending. Repeat the procedure to form the word *cat* by saying /ca/ as you tap your right shoulder, /t/ as you tap your left shoulder, and *cat* as you tap the middle of your chest. This can be repeated daily to foster students' blending skills.

Multisensory Blending

Materials Needed: none

At the Wilson Reading Program training for the instructional support specialists of the NYC Department of Education in August 2003, Barbara Wilson demonstrated a less conspicuous blending activity ideal for all ages. While sounding out the word *cat* touch your pointer finger to your thumb for /c/, your middle finger to your thumb for /a/, and your ring finger to your thumb for /t/. Then run your thumb over your fingers as you say the word *cat* aloud. Students can practice this under their desks as they read, thereby making this more practical for decoding work.

Blending Activities for Older Students

Materials Needed: flashcards with vowel-consonant and consonant-vowel-consonant letter combinations (see Appendix B for examples)

Students are shown flashcards with two letter vowel-consonant combinations. The students should say each individual sound aloud and then combine the sounds. It is important to begin with vowel-consonant combinations, since these are much easier to blend than CVC combinations.

Sound Boxes

Materials Needed: pictures of animals and objects with boxes underneath for each phoneme (not letter) in the word, colored chips or pennies

This task will require a good deal of modeling and guided instruction before the students can do this independently. Say the word slowly as you push the colored chips into each box, sound by sound. Use a different color for each sound. Be sure to stretch out the word enough so that you are pushing each chip into its box as the individual sound is being voiced.

Invented Spelling

Materials Needed: pencil and paper

Invented spelling is considered somewhat controversial, but this activity is simply to get students in the habit of isolating sounds. Encourage students to practice writing and try to guess how words are spelled. They will begin to have success as they learn to focus on identifying sounds and letter–sound correspondence. Once they have been taught a word, or letters that are contained in the word, it is no longer appropriate to accept invented spelling in their work.

LITERATURE-BASED ACTIVITIES

Super Syllable Man/Woman

Materials Needed: cape

When a child dons a cape in your classroom, he or she can become Super Syllable (Wo)Man (or Super Sound [Wo]Man if you decide to use this for onset/rimes or phonemes). During story time, choose words to break into syllables or sounds as you read. Super Syllable (Wo)Man should call out the word once he or she has correctly blended it together.

Blending During Reading

Materials Needed: Reading material

Decoding words is the key to understanding text, and students must apply the skills they have learned to guided and independent reading. When they find a word they do not know in any text, they should do the following:

1. Look at all the parts in the word, beginning with the first sound.
2. Look for word patterns they know.
3. Blend the sounds together.

Break It Up during Story Time

Materials Needed: storybook

At the end of a chapter or at the end of story time, pick a character's name or word from the story to segment and blend. Say the word, and then ask the students to repeat the word, segment it into sounds, and then blend it together. If the word is "Matt" the students should say "Matt, M-a-tt, Matt."

TRANSITION ACTIVITIES

Use these activities to move from one activity to another.

Follow My Directions

Materials Needed: none

We give children directions to follow many times during the day. Tell the children that when you give them a direction you are going to say one word in a silly way. The children must figure out the word in order to follow your direction.   Some examples may be:

Syllables and Compound Words

    Take out a pen-cil.
    Pass up your home-work.

Onsets and Rimes

    Last person on line, please close the d-oor
    Please put away your b-ooks.

Phonemes

    Carolyn, please get my k-ee-z.
    Take out a piece of p-a-p-er.

Hang up your c-oa-t-s.

Break It Up

Materials Needed: none

This is the same activity you can do after reading a story. The child repeats the word and segments each sound. If the word is *mug* then the student will repeat the word and then segment the word into m-u-g. The student then blends the word together again.

PHONEME
MANIPULATION

Phoneme manipulation is the final and most sophisticated level of phonemic awareness. In phoneme manipulation tasks, students are asked to isolate a sound in a word and then either delete it or move it in the word. They may be asked to replace one sound with another, or insert the sound in a different part of the word. For example, it could mean asking your students to change the word *lap* to *pal* or even change *slap* to *lasp*. This sort of activity requires a lot from the student, simultaneously tapping both memory and phonological skills.

Typically, phoneme manipulation is believed to be a second-grade skill. Researchers have found that fundamental spelling skills are a prerequisite to phoneme manipulation. In one study, researchers found that once an adequate level of letter recognition had been achieved, the ability to manipulate onsets and rimes in syllables related the most to reading achievement out of all the phonemic awareness skills. The combination of phoneme manipulation skills and phonics knowledge can only serve to build students' literacy skills.

This is why it is so important for students to get phonemic awareness instruction in tandem with a great amount of instruction and practice in reading and spelling. Initial decoding and phonemic awareness skills augment each other and are the most effective when they are developed simultaneously. This is not surprising, considering that students are being asked to think about and segment sounds before they can manipulate or delete them in words. Consonant blends are particularly difficult for students to segment, so you might want to spend extra time with this.

The activities in this chapter can be used for older or younger students unless specified otherwise. Some of the activities might feel too "babyish" to students past fourth grade. Use your judgment; if you feel an activity is too childish for your students feel free to modify it or skip it altogether.

CLASSROOM ACTIVITIES

Word Play

Materials Needed: monosyllabic nonsense words on a set of index cards (see Appendix B for sample list)

Show students each card and ask one student to segment the sounds in the word, such as *shap*. Once they have said "sh-a-p," ask them to change the word. One activity is to ask the students to change the vowel sound. Ask them to say the word and then say it again but change *a* to *i* and then *e*. Another activity is to remove the second sound in a blend, such as removing the *h* from *shap*, which would make the word *sap*. The students can also remove the beginning or ending sound from a word to create a new one. Finally, you can ask the students to say the word backward. We suggest that you try one activity per card.

Eat It

Materials Needed: a puppet, magnetic board with magnetic letters or a felt board with felt letters

Spell out a word using magnetic letters or felt letters. Introduce the puppet to the students. Tell the children that the puppet is very hungry and loves to eat letters. Have it eat the last letter in the word and ask the children to read what's left of the word.

Abracadabra

Materials Needed: a magic wand, a magician's hat (optional), magnetic letters or a dry erase board

You introduce this activity to the students by saying that something happened while you were sleeping last night. This morning you woke up and really wished that your annoying alarm clock would disappear. It suddenly disappeared, and now you think you gained magical powers in your sleep. You really want to try out your newfound magical powers. Spell out a word on the dry erase board or use magnetic letters. Tell the students that you are going to wave your magic wand over this word and it is going to become another word. Stand in front of the board (situate yourself so that you are covering the word) and wave your magic wand. While saying "Abracadabra" either substitute the initial sound with a new sound or delete it all together, then step back. Ask the children to read the new word.

The Name Game

Materials Needed: none

Arrange the children in a circle. One child begins by jumping over to the child next to him or her and substituting the initial sound in that child's name with the initial sound in his or her own name. For example, if Robert jumped over to Sue, Robert would have to say "Roo" and then Sue jumps over to Jack and Sue would have to say "Sack" and so on.

Leap Frog Letters

Materials Needed: letters signs

Choose two children to stand in front of the room with letters representing a spelling pattern. Each child represents one sound. The rest of the children have letter signs with the first letter of their name. They leap up to the word pattern children and say the sound of the letter they are holding. Then the whole class reads the word together. (Please note: some of the words derived may be nonsense words.)

Sound Mix-Up

Materials Needed: letter cards for students

Four students stand in front of the class, each holding a letter sign. If you choose the students holding the letters *s*, *p*, *i*, and *n*, ask them to form the word *spin*. Then ask them to change into the word *pins*. Then ask them to change into the word *nip*. Here are some possible words to work with:

Cast	(cats)
Spun	(pun, sun)
Stop	(pots, sop, spot, tops)
Star	(rats, tar, sat)
Grip	(rip, pig, rig)
Gum	(mug)
Fast	(fat, sat)
Part	(trap, rap, tap, tarp, tar)
Lamp	(map, Pam, pal)
Stamp	(Sam, mat, pat, tap, spat, past, mast)

Add a Sound

Materials Needed: white board or chart paper

In this activity, you are forming a word web, or graphic organizer. Put a two-letter word family, such as –an, in a circle on the board. Ask the students to give you consonants or blends that can go in front of the word pattern to make a word. For example, you could attach /sp/ and /t/ to the top of the circle or the sides to make the words *span* and *tan*, respectively. At the bottom, you can put /t/ and /d/ that could be added to the end of the pattern to form the words *ant* and *and*. The students should try attaching these sounds to the word pattern to create new words.

Make a Change (Older Student Activity)

Materials Needed: none

In this activity, you will start off with a word, such as *play*. You will say the word to a student. The student must change the word, either by adding, deleting, or substituting one of the sounds. For example, the student might say, "I'm taking out the /l/ and making the word *pay*." The next student could say, "I'm adding an /r/ sound and making the word into *pray*." If your students cannot think of a change to make, give them a suggestion by giving them a sound or telling them to delete a particular sound. They should then try to change the word based on your suggestion.

The Lokey Pokey

Materials Needed: blackboard

Tell the children that they are going to play a game in which they put letters in and out of words. Instead of playing the "Hokey Pokey," today they will be playing the "Lokey Pokey." Ask the children why they think it is called the "Lokey Pokey" instead of the "Hokey Pokey." Begin by writing the word *at* on the board. Then sing, "We put the *C* in, we put the *C* out, we put the *C* in and we sound the letters out. We do the Lokey Pokey and we turn ourselves around, and here's what the word spells out." The children then shout out the new word: *cat* (or you can point to one child to shout out the new word). Now change the initial sound to another letter, forming a new word. Sing, "We put the *C* in, we'll take the *C* out, we'll put an *F* in and we sound the letters out. We do the Lokey Pokey and we turn ourselves around, and here's what the word spells out." That is the children's cue to shout out the new word: *fat*.

For Consonant Blends

"We put the *L* in, we take the *L* out, we'll put the *L* in and we sound the letters out. We do the Lokey Pokey and we turn ourselves around, and here's what the word spells out." The children shout out the new word: *flat*.

Pig Latin (Older Student Activity)

Materials Needed: none

If you are teaching older students, begin by simply saying their names in Pig Latin. In Pig Latin, you take the initial sound off a word and put it at the end while attaching the /ay/ sound. For example, Margo is "Argomay" and Lynn is "Ynnlay" pronounced "Inlay." Once the students are comfortable speaking Pig Latin, they can progress to full sentences.

LITERATURE-BASED ACTIVITIES

Switching Sounds

Materials Needed: familiar and repetitive text

When reading a familiar text or poem aloud, have one child pick a letter he or she would like to use to substitute the initial sound of some of the title words. Begin by choosing only two or three words. For example, if the child chooses the letter *m*, *Alexander and the Terrible, Horrible, No Good, Very Bad Day* is read "Alexander and the terrible, horrible, no good, mery mad may." This will be repeated throughout the story by the class.

Further Suggestions

If the letter is *n*, *Harold and the Purple Crayon* becomes "Narold and the nurple nayon." If the letter is *t*, *Goodnight Moon* becomes "goodnight toon."

Deleting Sounds

Materials Needed: any story

When you're done reading a story to your students, repeat a sentence to them. Choose a word and ask them to delete a sound from that word. For example, if you're reading "Little Red Riding Hood" or the "Three Little Pigs," you can ask them to say the word *wolf*. Now say it again, but don't say /f/."

Variation: Try the same activity, but delete an initial sound.

TRANSITION ACTIVITIES

Use these activities to move from one activity to another.

Name of the Day

Materials Needed: none

While you are teaching phoneme manipulation, change your name to match the days of the week. If you are Ms. Jackson, on Monday mornings you become Ms. Mackson for the day. On Tuesdays you are Ms. Tackson, Wednesdays you are Ms. Wackson, Thursdays you are Ms. Thackson, and Fridays you are Ms. Fackson.

Variation: While going over the day's schedule, tell the children the following: "Today we are going to play 'Take Off the Beginning Sound.' As we move from one period to another I will tell you what materials we need for the next period. I want a volunteer to tell me the name of the material minus the first sound in the word. For example, if I say, 'Take out your paper' someone would say 'aper.'" "Everybody go to the rug" would become "ug." Try to use easy words so as not to confuse the students.

Add a Sound

Materials Needed: none

When it is time for the students to line up, ask them to add a sound to their name. Chris could be asked to add /p/ to his name and then becomes *Chrisp*.

APPENDIX A

TOOLS FOR
FURTHER ASSESSMENT

Crumrine, L., & Logan, H. (2000). *Phonological Awareness Skills Screening* (PASS). Chicago, IL: Applied Symbolix. Grades 1–2.

Rosner, J. (1975). *Test of Auditory Analysis Skills.* Navato, CA: Academic Therapy Publications. Grades 1–3.

Torgesen, J., & Bryant, B. (1997). *Test of Phonological Awareness* (TOPA). Austin, TX: PRO-ED, Inc. Grades K–2.

Torgesen, J. K., Wagner, R. K., & Rashotte, C. A. (1999). *Comprehensive Test of Phonological Processing.* Austin, TX: PRO-ED, Inc. Ages 5–6 and 7–24.

APPENDIX B

WORD LISTS
AND PATTERNS

COMPOUND WORDS

baseball	homework	snowball	snowman	classroom
airplane	dollhouse	playground	fireman	policeman
haircut	homerun	football	basketball	hairpin
sandbox	housework	dragonfly	skateboard	spaceship
broomstick	cheesecake	something	bedroom	everything
goldfish	newspaper	daydream	lunchroom	bedroom
cardboard	sunflower	flowerpot	scarecrow	tiptoe
something	anything	upstairs	downstairs	hallway
cupcake	bookcase	tabletop		

MULTISYLLABIC WORDS

One Syllable:	Two Syllables:	Three Syllables:	Four Syllables:
hair	paper	bubblegum	television
love	cookie	grasshopper	dictionary
witch	paper	frankfurter	calculator
man	pencil	hamburger	mathematics
plant	flower	telephone	obligation
gum	ketchup	furniture	unforgiving

One Syllable:	Two Syllables:	Three Syllables:	Four Syllables:
pen	window	computer	watermelon
book	sugar	magazine	participate
couch	carrot	history	firefighter
lamp	maintain	hypocrite	ridiculous
flag	toothpaste	terrific	January
soup	flashcard	happiness	underwater
glue	flashlight	highlighter	overactive
desk	sneakers	beautiful	pterodactyl

VC PATTERNS

(Use VC patterns as the first step for blending and segmenting nonsense words.)

at	in	em	on	us	ap	el	ut
am	it	ef	ot	ug	al	ej	ud
an	ig	es	os	um	ak	en	ub
ad	ip	ed	ol	un	ab	eb	om
ag	id	ev	og	up	od	op	ov

CVC AND CCVC PATTERNS FOR BLENDING NONSENSE WORDS

meg	ted	fled	ped	sent	gem	sheb	feb
crem	step	pelt	hesk	grel	drev	lesh	resp
flim	swig	hism	grid	slin	trig	prit	plig
kin	lid	stid	rit	plim	wig	fip	triv
tab	scap	pral	san	wag	jan	gran	chad
swam	maf	dwap	crag	gat	cad	blab	slap
blob	jost	skol	grom	kol	sop	losm	hog
bop	shon	tosp	drog	tod	loc	glob	wot
flun	swug	pust	mug	fuss	jurn	dwup	crub
lud	clum	pluk	srut	jult	brug	gull	bup

ONSETS AND RIMES

For onsets and rimes, we recommend using high-frequency word patterns (rimes) with the following endings:

ack	ap	it	op
uck	in	est	ot
ink	an	ell	eat
at	ick	ing	ock

Add consonants and blends to these patterns, so students learn to recognize word patterns as they segment and blend onsets and rimes.

APPENDIX C

CHILDREN'S LITERATURE RECOMMENDATIONS

Ahlberg, J., & Ahlberg, A. (1978). *Each peach pear plum*. New York: Scholastic.

Andreae, G. (1999). *Cock-a-doodle-doo! Barnyard hullabaloo*. New York: Scholastic.

Banker, B. (2000). *Silly songs for phonology and sound awareness*. Eau Claire, WI: Thinking Publications.

Beall, P., & Nipp, S. (1986). *Wee sing— Children's songs & fingerplays*. New York: Putnam & Grosset Group.

Brown, M. W. (1996). *Goodnight moon*. New York: Harper Trophy.

Calmenson, S. (1993). *It begins with an A*. New York: Hyperion Books for Children.

Carle, E. (1974). *The very hungry caterpillar*. Markham, ON: Penguin Puffin Press.

Clements, A. (1997). *Double trouble in Walla Walla*. Brookfield, CT: Millbrook Press.

Ernst, L. C. (1996). *The letters are lost*. New York: Scholastic.

Handford, M. (1997). *Where's Waldo?* Cambridge, MA: Candlewick Press.

Hoberman, M. A. (1998). *Miss Mary Mack*. New York: Scholastic.

Hoberman, M. A. (2001). *There once was a man named Michael Finnegan*. Boston: Little, Brown.

Jackson, A. (1997). *I know an old lady who swallowed a pie*. New York: Scholastic.

Johnson, C. (1981). *Harold and the purple crayon.* New York: Harper-Collins.

Keats, E. J. (1962). *The snowy day.* New York: Viking.

Lippman, S., Kaye, B., & Wise, F. (1991). *A you're adorable.* Cambridge, MA: Candlewick Press.

Lyne, A. (1997). *A my name is.* New York: Scholastic.

Martin, Jr., B. (1992). *Brown bear, brown bear, what do you see?* New York: Henry Holt.

Marzollo, J., & Wick, W. (1995). *I spy school days: A book of picture riddles.* New York: Scholastic.

Rifkin, J. (2001). *The everything Mother Goose book.* Holbrook, MA: Adams Media.

Scarry, R. (1970). *Richard Scarry's best Mother Goose ever.* New York: Western.

Sendak, M. (1963). *Where the wild things are.* New York: HarperCollins.

Sendak, M. (1991). *Chicken soup with rice.* New York: Harper Trophy.

Seuss, Dr. (1996). *Dr. Seuss's ABC: An amazing alphabet book.* New York: Random House.

Seuss, Dr. (1996). *There's a wocket in my pocket.* New York: Random House Children's Books.

Silverstein, S. (1974). *Where the sidewalk ends: Poems and drawings.* New York: Harper & Row.

Slepian, J., & Seidler, A. (2001). *The hungry thing.* Chicago: Follett.

Slobodkina, E. (1987). *Caps for sale.* New York: Harper Trophy.

There was an old lady who swallowed a fly. (2000). Auburn, ME: Child's Play (International).

Trapani, I. (1993). *The itsy bitsy spider.* Dallas: Whispering Coyote Press.

Trapani, I. (1996). *I'm a little teapot.* New York: Scholastic.

Viorst, J. (1987). *Alexander and the terrible, horrible, no good, very bad day.* New York: Aladdin Books/Macmillan Publishers.

Weinberg, L. (1982). *Guess a rhyme.* New York: Random House.

Young, R. (1992). *Golden bear.* New York: Viking

REFERENCES

Adams, M. J. (1990). *Beginning to read—Thinking and learning about print*. Cambridge, MA: MIT Press.

Adams, M. J., Foorman, B. R., Lundberg, I., & Beeler, T. (1998). *Phonemic awareness in young children: A classroom curriculum*. Baltimore: Brookes.

Bryant, P., MacLean, M., & Bradley, L. (1990). Rhyme, language, and children's reading. *Applied Psycholinguistics, 11,* 237–252.

Carroll, D. W. (1999). *The psychology of language*. Pacific Grove, CA: Brooks/Cole.

Carroll, J. M., & Snowling, M. J. (2001). The effects of global similarity between stimuli on children's judgment of rime and alliteration. *Applied Pyscholinguistics, 22,* 327–342.

Catts, H., & Olsen, T. (1993*). Sounds abound.* East Moline, IL: LinguiSystems.

Chafouleas, S. M., Lewandowski, L. J., Smith, C. R., & Blachman, B. A. (1997). Phonological awareness skills in children: Examining performance across tasks and ages. *Journal of Psychoeducational Assessment, 15,* 334–347.

Chall, J. S. (1983). *Stages of reading development*. New York: McGraw-Hill.

Clay, M. (2000). *Reading recovery: A guide for teachers in training*. Portsmouth, NH: Heinemann.

Cox, A. (1992). *Foundations for literacy*. Cambridge, MA: Educational Publishing Service.

Crane, K., & Law, K. (2002). *Preparing to read: Easy-to-use phonological awareness activities*. Westminster, CA: Creative Teaching Press.

Cunningham, J. W., Cunningham, P. M., Hoffman, J. V., & Yopp, H. K. (1998). *Phonemic awareness and the teaching of reading: A position statement from the board of directors of the International Reading Association*. Newark, DE: International Reading Association.

Cunningham, P. M. (2000). *Phonics they use: Words for reading and writing*. New York: Longman.

Ehri, L. C. (1996). Phases of word learning: Implications for instruction with delayed and disabled readers. *Reading and Writing Quarterly: Overcoming Learning Difficulties, 14*, 136–168.

Ericson, L., & Juliebo, M. F. (1998). *The phonological awareness handbook for kindergarten and primary teachers*. Newark, DE: International Reading Association.

Goswami, U. (2002). Phonology, reading development and dyslexia: A cross-linguistic perspective. *Annals of Dyslexia, 52*, 1–23.

Griffin, P. L., & Olson, M. W. (1992). Phonemic awareness helps beginning readers break the code. *Reading Teacher, 45*(7), 516–523.

Hajdusiewicz, B. B. (1998). *Phonics through poetry: Teaching phonemic awareness using poetry*. Glenview, IL: Goodyear.

Johns, J., & Lenski, S. D. (1997). *Improving reading: A handbook of strategies*. Dubuque, IA: Kendall/Hunt.

Kaye, P. (1984). *Games for reading*. New York: Pantheon.

Lachance, S. (2002). *Sounds abound storybook activities*. East Moline, IL: LinguiSystems (1-800 PRO IDEA).

Lipson, M. Y., & Wixon, K. K. (1997). *Assessment and instruction of reading and writing disability; an interactive approach* (2nd ed.). New York: Addison Wesley Longman.

Maclean, M., Bryant, P., & Bradley, L. (1987). Rhymes, nursery rhymes, and reading in early childhood. *Merrill-Palmer Quarterly, 33*(3), 255–281.

McBride-Chang, C. (1995). What is phonological awareness? *Journal of Educational Psychology, 87*(2), 179–192.

Moats, L. C., & Farrell, M. L. (1999). Multisensory instruction. In J. R. Birsch (Ed.), *Multisensory teaching of basic language skills* (pp. 1–18). Baltimore: Paul H. Brookes.

Nation, K., & Hulme, C. (1997). Phonemic segmentation, not onset-rime segmentation, predicts early reading and spelling skills. *Reading Research Quarterly, 32*, 154–167.

Richards, R. G. (1999). *The source for dyslexia and dysgraphia*. East Moline, IL: LinguiSystems.

Snow, C. E., Burns, M. S., & Griffin, P. (Eds.). (1998). *Preventing reading difficulties in young children*. Washington, DC: National Academy Press.

Snowling, M. (2000). *Dyslexia*. Oxford, Eng.: Blackwell.

Stahl, S. A., & Murray, B. A. (1994). Defining phonological awareness and its relationship to early reading. *Journal of Educational Psychology, 86*(2), 221–234.

Uhry, J. K. (1999). Phonological awareness and reading: Research, activities, and instructional materials. In J. R. Birsch (Ed.), *Multisensory teaching of basic language skills* (pp. 63–84). Baltimore: Paul H. Brookes.

Walley, A. (1988). The role of vocabulary development in children's spoken word recognition and segmentation ability. *Developmental Review, 13*, 145–167.

Whitehurst, G. J., & Lonigan, C. J. (1998). Child development and emergent literacy. *Child Development, 69*, 848–872.

Yopp, H. K., & Yopp, R. H. (2000). Supporting phonemic awareness development in the classroom. *Reading Teacher, 54*(2), 130–143.

INDEX

ABOUT THE AUTHORS

Lynn Settlow received an M.A. from Teachers College, Columbia University, as a reading specialist. She is the high school reading specialist for the Churchill School in New York City.

Margarita Jacovino received an M.S. in education of the speech and hearing handicapped from Brooklyn College. She has worked as a speech and language service provider for 9 years. She is an elementary school instructional support specialist for the New York City Department of Education.